Partes de
la planta
Plant Parts

¿Por qué las plantas tienen semillas?

Why Do Plants Have Seeds?

Celeste Bishop

Traducido por Eida de la Vega

PowerKiDS
press.

New York

Published in 2016 by The Rosen Publishing Group, Inc.
29 East 21st Street, New York, NY 10010

First Edition

Editor: Sarah Machajewski
Book Design: Mickey Harmon
Translator: Eida de la Vega

Photo Credits: Cover, p. 22 (dandelions) Brian A Jackson/Shutterstock.com; cover, p. 1 (logo, frame) Perfect Vectors/Shutterstock.com; cover, pp. 1, 3–4, 7–8, 11–12, 15–16, 19–20, 23–24 (background) djgis/Shutterstock.com; p. 5 EM Arts/Shutterstock.com; p. 6 designelements/Shutterstock.com; p. 9 TADDEUS/Shutterstock.com; pp. 10, 17 Nigel Cattlin/Visuals Unlimited/Getty Images; p. 13 (inset) Grygoril Lykhatskyi/Shutterstock.com; p. 13 (main) Edouard Coleman/Shutterstock.com; © iStockphoto.com/ClarkandCompany; p. 18 (sky) Evgeny Karadaev/Shutterstock.com; p. 18 (plant) Bogdan Wankowicz/Shutterstock.com; p. 21 oksana2010/Shutterstock.com.

Cataloging-in-Publication Data

Bishop, Celeste, author.
 Why do plants have seeds? = ¿Por qué las plantas tienen semillas? / Celeste Bishop.
    pages cm. — (Plant parts = Partes de la planta)
Parallel title: Partes de la planta.
In English and Spanish.
 Includes index.
 ISBN 978-1-5081-4732-9 (library binding)
 1. Seeds—Juvenile literature. 2. Plants—Juvenile literature. I. Title.
 QK661.B57 2016
 575.6'8—dc23

Manufactured in the United States of America

CPSIA Compliance Information: Batch #BW16PK: For Further Information contact Rosen Publishing, New York, New York at 1-800-237-9932

Contenido / Contents

- -

Mira este objeto. ¿Sabes lo que es? ¡Es una semilla!

Look at this object. Do you know what it is? It's a seed!

Una semilla es una parte importante de la planta. Es donde comienza la vida de la planta.

- -

A seed is a very important plant part. It is where a plant's life begins.

La capa dura de una semilla se llama **tegumento**. El tegumento protege el interior de la semilla.

A seed's hard covering is called a **seed coat**. The seed coat keeps the inside of the seed safe.

tegumento / seed coat

9

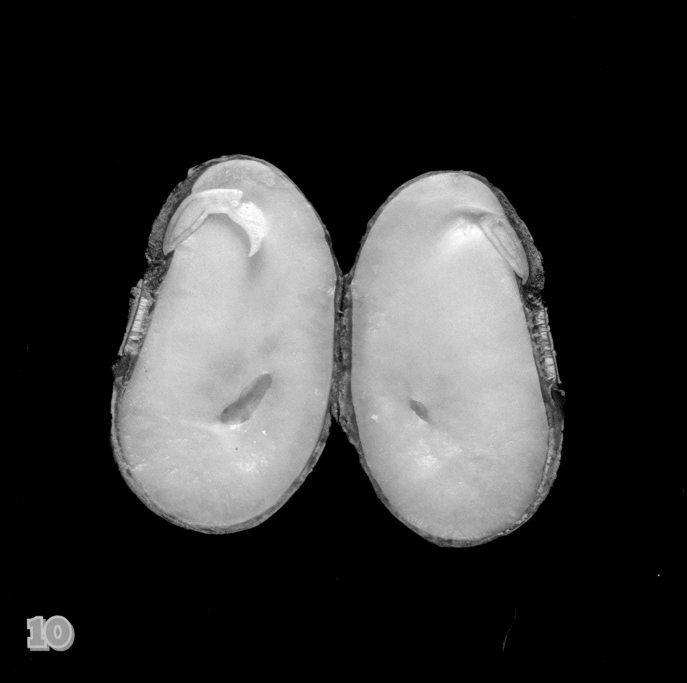

El interior de una semilla
contiene una planta bebé
y su alimento. Una planta
necesita de ambos para crecer.

The inside of a seed holds
a baby plant and its food.
A plant needs both to grow.

Algunas plantas forman semillas dentro de las flores. Otras plantas forman semillas dentro del **fruto**.

Some plants form seeds inside their flowers. Other plants form seeds inside their **fruit**.

semillas / seeds

13

Las semillas se plantan en la tierra. Las semillas necesitan agua, luz del sol y aire para crecer.

Seeds are planted in the ground. Seeds need water, sunlight, and air to grow.

¿Qué sucede cuando una semilla empieza a crecer? La planta bebé rompe el tegumento de la semilla.

What happens when a seed starts to grow? The baby plant breaks out of the seed coat.

planta
plant

raíces
roots

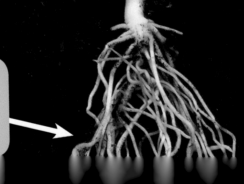

Partes de la planta bebé crecen hacia abajo. Esas son las **raíces**. El resto de la planta crece hacia arriba.

Parts of the baby plant grow down. These are the **roots**. The rest of the plant grows up.

Cuando la planta crece,
nacen nuevas semillas.

When the plant is fully grown,
it makes new seeds.

21

El viento transporta las semillas a nuevos lugares. Los animales y las personas también pueden transportar las semillas. ¡Y así crecen nuevas plantas!

The wind carries seeds to new places. Animals and people can carry seeds, too.
Then, new plants grow!

PALABRAS QUE DEBES APRENDER / WORDS TO KNOW

(el) fruto /
fruit

(las) raíces /
roots

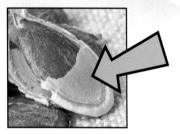

(el) tegumento /
seed coat

ÍNDICE / INDEX

SITIOS DE INTERNET / WEBSITES

Due to the changing nature of Internet links, PowerKids Press has developed an online list of websites related to the subject of this book. This site is updated regularly. Please use this link to access the list: www.powerkidslinks.com/part/seed

24